52 Views

The Haibun Variations

52 Views

The Haibun Variations

JIM NATAL

TEBOT BACH • HUNTINGTON BEACH • CALIFORNIA 2013

ACKNOWLEDGMENTS

The *haibun* below have appeared, sometimes in slightly different forms, in the following print and online journals:

Hotel Amerika: "Clothes shopping with my wife" and "I'm watching my cat"
In Posse: "An ad on late night TV" and "Wide awake at 3 AM"
Spillway: "An NFL head coach," "NPR reports," and "Two cannonballs"

"Preparing for winter" (as "Do it Yourself") appears in the anthology
In the Black/In the Red (Helicon Nine Editions, 2013)

Special thanks to Susan Terris, David St. John, and Carla Riedel for their suggestions, continued encouragement, and friendship, and to my sisters, Barbara, Judy, and Jane.

Book Cover Art: Joe Goode, "Untitled" (Torn Cloud Series), 1974.
   Joe Goode Studio.

Book Design & Layout: Tania Baban

ISBN 13: 978-1-893670-94-5
ISBN 10: 1-893670-94-5

Library of Congress Control Number: 2013935194

Manufactured in the United States of America

A Tebot Bach book

Tebot Bach, Welsh for little teapot, is A Nonprofit Public Benefit Corporation which sponsors workshops, forums, lectures, and publications. Tebot Bach books are distributed by Small Press Distribution, Armadillo and Ingram.

The Tebot Bach Mission: advancing literacy, strengthening community, and transforming life experiences with the power of poetry through readings, workshops, and publications.

www.tebotbach.org

Always for Tania

TABLE OF CONTENTS

A BRIEF INTRODUCTION

This collection of poems written in the *haibun* form has nothing to do with Japan, and yet it has everything to do with Bashō, Hokusai, Mt. Fuji, and Kyoto's Philosopher's Walk (as explained in the "Afterword"). *Haibun*, very simply defined, are brief blocks of prose—not prose poetry—accompanied by, and interacting in some way with, a commentary haiku-like poem. If written skillfully, the haiku reflects back upon the prose and shades its meaning and the subject experience in a new way. What appears here in *52 Views* is only an interpretation of the *haibun* form run through my coarse American filter. In other words, these are not classic *haibun*, with all the inherent Japanese cultural subtleties and references, but simply my take on the form. The individual *haibun* are untitled; they use a portion of the first line for "Table of Contents" purposes. And though there are only a few direct mentions of things Japanese in these poems, the work is infused with my appreciation of the mystique of Japanese poetry and art. Without it, this book would never have become anything except another bad case of evanescence ●

Written on my summer fan
torn in half
in autumn

Matsuo Bashō

*P*reparing for winter, work moves indoors. Paint the spare bedroom: three walls and the ceiling off-white; contrast one wall and closet door café-au-lait (as if you could drink the paint). The rollers suck it up; layers accumulate like years, color upon color, covering those that came before, sometimes dark over light. I hope this won't be like Po Chu-i's poem, "A Guest Doesn't Come," the host alone beside the front gate at dawn. Blue masking tape wadded into sticky planets. Soak the brushes used for trim. Bigger projects put off until spring. Maybe things will be better then.

Every month bills.
Wealth migrates like certain birds—
wait for their return.

I had to bring in the potted cacti and the ficus. The temperature will drop into the 20s tonight; they might not survive, black spots on the waxy barrels, leaves cringed brown. Even given my lethargy when it comes to home and garden chores, I can't let a spring and summer's worth of growth spurts go to waste. They'll spend the winter in the garage, where they lean toward the little east-facing window straining for the wan early sun. If their efforts were audible it probably would sound like someone sucking the last drops of a take-out drink through a straw. Living takes such effort and will. A friend just had a brain tumor removed, the most recent in a procession of treatments and surgeries. She tells me cancer patients have a different sense of time, more urgency to everything. I am in awe of her strength and spirit. In her place I would have shriveled.

Autumn gardening,
removing dead leaves caught in spines;
hand not to get pricked.

A winter solstice snow squall rattles and speckles the glass. I should have sealed the windows as my neighbor suggested months ago. But he used to be a contractor, understands drywall and caulk, doesn't have his manhood tested every trip to the hardware store; aisles of questions and work I don't know how to do, shelves of metal implements whose shapes give no sense of purpose. I am truly my father's son, five thumbs on each hand—stripped screws and crooked nails. Maybe I can fill the chinks with poems, put them to practical use.

To sharpen and hone,
words fine as Damascus steel;
my poetry tools.

"Two cannonballs were eating a clown." At least that's what I thought I heard in my early-morning doze. But in the next radio cycle I found out it was a joke: "Two *cannibals* were eating a clown. One says to the other: 'Does this taste funny to you?'" Then came another story of devastation, misery, and indefensible loss of life in Afghanistan, Iraq, or was it Gaza this time? The casualties were not collateral clowns but they were eaten just the same by cannibals in uniform, consumed by cannonballs' contemporary equivalents: IEDs, drones, cheap AKs, cluster bombs, bouncing mines, RPGs. A human mind thought them up; the punch lines knock 'em dead. Imagine: no electricity for weeks, no medical assistance allowed into the zones, lying awake in the dark with wounds oozing, burns crusting over, families alternating between wailing and cursing. Oversize footfalls sound in halls of bullet-pocked buildings...

Death pounds door-to-door—
white make up, bulb nose, huge shoes,
bloated red buttons.

My wife and I down with infection. Everything becomes surfaces—the surfaces we touch and that touch us. Counters, handles, clothing, bedding, towels. Our own skin. How many times we touch ourselves; how much we want to touch each other. Soap, disinfectant, wipes, tissues—such thin films to protect us from the pathogenic invisible. We read up on our condition. Anxieties build at case histories—misdiagnosis, delayed diagnosis, chronic recurrence, resistance to treatment, chancy surgery, and death. I become sensitized to stories of suffering and they are *everywhere!* Buddha's first noble truth of life prevails. Our affliction came out of nowhere, and like all misery that humans must bear, it will be gone. I tell my wife incessantly how much I love her. Any little thing can take it.

Sweeping second hand;
people hang on, spin around,
drop off one by one.

I 'm watching my cat watch a jackrabbit through the window behind my computer. Giant pink ears sticking out above the rough high desert vegetation as it browses, unaware of us, yet totally alert. Who is watching me watch them, oblivious to the dimensions over my shoulder, predators just beyond reach of the corner of my eye?

Arabic saying:
Be wolf or wolves will eat you.
Natural order.

An empty feeder;
hummingbird perched in the snow.
Why didn't you fly?

This is the time of reduced expectations. It has nothing to do with the weather, although I hear it's wreaking havoc on crops around the world. Drought in one place, flooding in another, and now the cold comes on. Food shortages engender riots, hoarding in countries that can afford it. And everyone struggling with money. When countries can't pay their bills they print more. When people can't pay their bills they make do with less and less and then less. No longer prayers for frivolous wealth. Please, oh Lord, keep us solvent, sheltered, and fed.

How do they survive
in winter without flowers?
Even bugs stay in.

Winter storm warnings and dire economic warnings from our president. Snow comes down. The stock market comes down. Only the wind picks up; big fat flakes blowing sideways while Congress pedals furiously on its stationary bike. By late afternoon the snow begins to stick. And by evening, accumulation. School closures announced for tomorrow morning, a rare snow day. Drifts against the mock adobe walls. Branches sag, trees arranged like art installations, bushes just white humps sitting still as rabbits in the dark. The wind has died. Somewhere there is snow in both stirrups.

Bitter cold morning.
We rise early, catch moonlight
in bed with the snow.

nderwater. As if there's been a catastrophic flood. As if we're living in the backfill aftermath of the construction of a massive dam, watching appraised values submerge like towns. We're so deep now we need scuba tanks to view the sunken ruins. At least I've got a roof over my head. My dead father, who went through the Great Depression, would say something like that. Now I've got a house and a depression of my own. And a roof over my head that leaks when the snowmelt begins. We put pinging pots out to catch the drips like Ma and Pa Kettle. Be thankful you've got a pot to piss in, my father whispers. He's far beyond this. Dad, you can put all the béarnaise sauce you want on a shit sandwich. It's still a shit sandwich.

Oh, Evanescence!
I wrote you a lovely song...
except now it's gone.

*I*n Santa Fe at Christmastime, *farolitos* line the walks and glow on ramparts of adobe walls, burning candles set in brown paper bags filled with sand, tops folded down like knee socks. Now there are *electrolitos*, new traplines of wired plastic facsimiles. The chilly dusk gifts us the unmistakable scent of piñon smoke, for which there is no battery-powered equivalent. The art is expensive on Canyon Road, where Seattle billionaires buy paintings in bulk, even as public arts funding is frozen. But the almost-full moon is not yet for sale rising through barren conifer branches. And the distant snowcaps still offer the colors of sunset at cost. Outside a gallery there's a sculpture of three dancing pigs. They wear red wool scarves, feel no cold.

The spirit warned Scrooge:
Beware Want and Ignorance.
Winter knows neither.

The two most expensive words in American English are "starting at," followed by a dollar sign. No matter how low the come-on cost, once the extras are factored-in the final price is always double. Everybody knows, as Leonard Cohen sings, the dice are loaded, the fight was fixed, and the deal was rotten. Maybe it's a fact of my latent Jewishness or the red tide of national anxiety, but I never go to bed expecting that I, my loved ones, and the details of my life—my home, my assets, my work, my plans, even my destinations—will be there in the morning.

Grasp security
as if this world were solid.
Nothing's what it seems.

*O*n the last morning of the year I'm having poetry and jasmine tea in bed, beneath the weight of blankets and last night's phone message from a dear friend (ovarian cancer, stage four). The "Goldberg Variations" play and play. My 73-year-old best friend calls to tell me his marriage is failing. They can't agree on the temperature of the house. He's freezing to death, he says, can't take it anymore. He's survived great pain and a nearly fatal car crash in a distant country. His fight sounds gone, used up. Then my sister calls. She's losing her job after 19 years. She suspected it was coming and here it is. We tell stories, we write poems to try to explain it to ourselves. What else can we do?

One tree on a hill,
caws of invisible crows.
Then it starts to snow.

Wide awake at 3 AM, the stars drew me out of bed. It was one of those cosmic canopies that occur only on the clearest, coldest nights. I raised the blinds and half expected to see the Aurora Borealis as if this were Alaska. At the point the star show became too strong to resist, I had been lying there fantasizing that my old dog had come back to visit me in the night, his face close to mine at the edge of the bed, big nose cold against my bare shoulder. I reached out from under the quilt to touch fur, so palpable was my envisioning—or maybe my longing. But, of course, he wasn't there. The way my father is never there when I seek his advice. He never offered much when he was alive. Just example. Maybe I never really asked, or he sensed that what I required was not his opinion but to make my own decisions. Either way, there were two parallel stars shining at equal intensity just above the juniper trees and, although there were multitudes of others, I couldn't keep from returning their stare.

Expands and contracts,
that nameless constellation;
light years between breaths.

Rwandan coffee this morning, grounds dark as fertile soil. Bought for flavor, but also out of pity, to show economic compassion for those woeful people who suffered so much and so long at each other's hands. The package carries a description as for wine: medium body, brown sugar aroma with an herbal complexity; but I can't catch any hints of the promised sweet orange. What I do taste—and, of course, this is only me very early in the morning—is blood, a tint of copper on the tip of my tongue. Am I drinking traces of the spill caused by some Hutu or Tutsi machete? Are there coffee cooperatives that hire only one-armed pickers? I cradle my cup and look outside. Another clear, sunny Arizona sky, equatorial heat without the humidity. The finches strafe the feeder and the ants form up into convoy lines. It's so quiet here—never even the slightest echo of horrible strife.

Grinding coffee beans,
last night's qualms through the filter;
first liquid, then steam.

We've been given a date for the Afghan pull-out. As if the moment the final NATO transport is airborne the patient tide won't roll back in. My money's on the fundamentalists of any stripe—skullcaps and *keffiyehs,* black frock coats, spotless *dishdashas*—all so afraid of pleasure boats cruising the birth canal. The new dark ages are upon us, gaining momentum like a runaway midnight express, its one bright eye tightly closed. And the rustlings in dawn branches? Only crows. Vultures and crows.

Dormant in the snow
yuccas await their moment,
ruthless in their faith.

*J*ust when you think it's over—*wham!*—another snowstorm hits. I learned not to be lulled years ago growing up in Chicago, where they say it isn't really spring until the dog poop melts out from under the elms. We've had a run of days in the 50s and 60s. But I knew better than to put away the sweaters. When I complain about winter dragging on to my sister back home—where the wind chill factor was born and you can go for weeks without seeing the sun, where everything is sooty brick and shades of drab gray and brown—she cheerily reminds me of her favorite of my mother's winter sayings: *Nobody cares what you look like when it snows.*

The gibbous moon breaks,
casts a shadow, then sees it.
Winter six more weeks.

I want to make an apology 50 years too late. To Ralphie, my high school football coach. I loathed you, thought you were the stupidest Polack on earth. But now I have to admit: you were right. It all comes down to "Ya gotta wanna." And you were right about something else: I didn't "block wort' a fiddle." The south side of Chicago was a tough place to play football and, given my size, offensive guard was the wrong position for me, number 49, looking up from my stance at 20-year-old 300-pounders blotting out the autumn sun. I know you wanted me to challenge you, to argue, so you could kick my ass in front of the team. But I never did. If you had seen me play on Sundays in the touch league you may have changed your mind. I was an all-star, got to carry the ball, and it was a rougher game than tackle. No equipment, just body to body at speed; elbows, shoulders, knees. But that doesn't change the fact of your…I'll call it wisdom. I'm past 60, a poet, father, and teacher and, yes, abso-freakin'-lutely, Ralphie, *ya gotta wanna.*

Dawn recollections,
flying birds in retrospect;
egrets, not regrets.

I see my mother in my sisters. I see my father in myself, in the things I say, the way I say them and when. Sometimes the distinctions fade. I watch the onset of old age; my body disappoints and is shameless in its surrender. Mirrors murmur to mirrors: *But I don't feel old inside.* My mother used to say that. How could I believe her then; varicose veins, skin hanging, memory slipping out under the door like oxygen sucked away by a fire in the next room? I used to think she was only trying to convince herself.

Those winter clichés
about aging and the trees.
We adapt. We lie.

At a party my petite wife Tania is cornered by a stranger who wants to know her origins. Maybe he's detected the slight accent in her flawless English. Or perhaps it's her Mediterranean olive skin and dark brown eyes. "You're not from here," he says. When she tells him she grew up in Beirut, she becomes to him an instant expert on the Middle East, challenged to defend the actions of those she hasn't lived among for more than 30 years. This is not the first time. In fact, it seems to be happening more frequently as two wars drag on and people here, where diversity is a foreign concept, fledge more right wings. "I'm sick and tired of it," she fumes. "Next time I'll say I'm from Argentina."

No monkey on his
back, this one; a curious
cat on his shoulder.

March madness is in the air. The swallows are expected back in southern California, their imminent arrival announced with festival banners strung across the *avenidas* of San Juan Capistrano, prompting images of kindly mission friars in brown burlap, halos of little Disney birds darting around their tonsured heads. In fitting contrast, the turkey vultures have returned to northern Arizona. God's ugliest angels, who vomit in self-defense. I didn't even know they migrated south. Short of a cartel gang, it's hard to imagine a more gruesome congregation around a Mexican resort pool. But try to think of vultures as a service-oriented species and the finest example of semiotics in nature: see a circle in the sky and you know something's dead.

Spring taking its time,
even the sun's impatient.
Where's that Tanager?

*P*alm trees and Malibu on television last night. We mostly get L.A.'s hand-me-down weather, can actually watch the clouds troubling in from the coast, gaining momentum across the desert mountains. I love how people say that L.A. has no seasons. Sure it does. They're just different: fog, beach, fire, a month or so of rain followed by mudslides, a few consecutive nights in the 40s that stand-in for winter. And, of course, there are earthquakes. But they jump the line, make their own calendar.

Buried bulbs rousing;
adept as celebrities
at reinvention.

I saw the cherry blossoms in Kyoto almost exactly a year ago; the spring before that in D.C.— enthralling beyond obvious metaphor. The Japanese regard their trees with such ancient reverence, roots intertwined over the centuries, inspiring master poets to their finest haiku. Rituals are celebrated, family picnics in the Emperor's gardens, couples strolling hand-in-hand in pink drifts, copious photos taken. But late March brings as much anxiety as sense of renewal for those born in snow country. Yesterday, we found a single bud opening on the skeletal pear tree beside our driveway. Just that one white flower among all the branches of all the trees. How does it know the moment?

Foolhardy blossom,
protruding nail on bare branch.
Please, no hammer frost.

The Indian Ocean run hard aground; Haiti and New Zealand. Then Japan's earthquake and hellhound tsunami—Hokusai's wave finally crashed. Seawater sludge chocked with cars and boats, buildings and bodies. Who wasn't struck dumb by the freight train inundation of villages on the shoreline, of higher ground that wasn't high enough? Whose heart didn't reach out for those too slow up the bluffs burdened with family members or possessions, those who stayed, who went back? It was a causal nexus on a macro scale: catastrophic failure of containment vessels and cooling pools, explosions and unquenchable fires, toxic steam and violated *nori* beds—devastation that Godzilla, Rodan, and Mothra together couldn't have wrought. And the aftershocks of lies, bribes, ass-coverings, and face-savings are just beginning. I went through the '94 Northridge quake in southern California, twenty seconds of forever. Tohoku's lasted longer and was exponentially stronger. Maybe the ancients were right and all the movies have been wrong. It's not Earth *vs.* the Monsters. It's Earth *vs.* us.

Horse by split rail fence,
flanks quiver, ripple, and twitch.
Pestilent flies, off!

An ad on late night TV touts a new "Girls Gone Wild" video: *50 Best Breasts Ever!* Despite my poetic admiration for the title's internal rhyme and alliteration, I mull a question—does the video feature 50 girls or just 25? You know, truth in advertising. Bowing to network proprieties, the sample footage features grayed-out swatches across the chests and pubic regions of the oh-so-perky participants, reminiscent of the black bars across eyes in retro "dirty" magazines. One girl (and these *are* girls) flips up the top of her bikini; her breasts leap at the camera like, you know, beasts gone wild. Another girl on what appears to be an RV bed declares, "I am the hottest girl in America," a claim that might be disputed by the other 49 (or 24) subjects. These girls could be my daughter's college roommates…or my daughter. How many fathers, in the interest of research, have gone so far as to order? Which sets up an interesting premise: suppose the girl gone wild is yours?

Breast fascination—
amazing how it changes:
wife's radiation.

My student writes about his last day in Iraq, the one that ends with his getting blown up by an IED. I try to separate form from content the way the insurgent separated my student from much of his blood and nearly his life. His essay needs a lot of work—spelling, punctuation, flow. *Point and support, point and support,* I drone to the class. No argument without example. No blast without detonation.

The rules of grammar,
dispassionate as a bomb;
each wire connected.

An NFL head coach, famous for his malapropisms, once talked about motivation, what he called "the carrot at the end of the tunnel." Actually, that's not such a wacky description, as long as you consider this life to be a straight-line journey. We enter the world through a tunnel and, if the consensus of near-death survivors is to be believed, we depart through one as well. *Go toward the white light* and hope it's not an oncoming cosmology. But re the carrot: there's the question of how long it will dangle sufficient allure to pursue it. At some point it has to dawn on even the dumbest of asses that he's not gonna get that carrot unless his owner gives it to him. Ask any assembly line stiff or drone in a corporate tower and most will tell you that at some point they realized the chase just isn't worth the effort. Maybe suicides would, too, if they could; you can quit existing the same as quitting a job, though you can always get another job. Well, these days maybe not. It just depends on how much you want that carrot and what you're willing to put up with to get it. After all, to quote the same NFL coach, "This isn't rocket surgery."

Old Lao Tzu chides:
the race, the hunt, drives men mad.
Cold rain calls "Time out."

ome repair hell continues this week. Listening to Otis Rush sing the blues: "Ain't enough money comin' in to take care of what's got to go out." Roof repairs, deck repairs, plaster and plumbing, proactive weed control, and, as a late add to the money pit roster, parapet reconstruction on the top edges of our Santa Fe-style house; pray there's no interior water damage from leaks caused by the record winter storms. (Note to self: *Never* buy a flat-roof house again.) We're discovering too late how much we underestimated the unending maintenance endemic to this region. But extreme weather is suddenly everywhere—the coldest this, the hottest that, the wettest, the driest, tornadoes and hurricanes way out of season. Yet naysayers insist there's no such thing as climate change; just keep their heads down, thumb their bibles.

Spring re-emergence,
blinking in the April sun:
You homeowner fool...

At dinner with a colleague, we try to come up with a one-line description of the difference between poetry and prose. Imagery, precision, and concision come up, as does the fact that poetry works more in your head than on the page. We decide that poetry captures the "essence" of an experience. The next night, a fiction-writer friend tells me of issues with his new book contract, his agent's snit over royalties. In poetry, I say, the definition of royalty has to do with kings and queens. Welcome to the lucrative multi-million-dollar poetry industry. Who needs a full line when one word will suffice: the difference between poetry and prose is "money."

Ground too hard to break;
the shoot and root don't know that,
do it anyway.

Some days in this life I'd like to make a *Five Easy Pieces* exit; give my wallet to my wife, say "I'll be right back." Then hitch a ride with a semi going the other way. But I'm no Nicholson, could never sneer at a waitress to hold the tomato "between yer knees" or take advantage of poor Rayette in her pert pink uniform, who, though she doesn't know much, knows she's the only one who'll ever love me the way she does. My wife loves me. I know that. My daughter, too. I'm not so sure about my cat.

In Yiddish they say,
I release you, release you;
Death, Taxes, Divorce.

All the trees are blooming and popping leaves; I can almost hear them, like little green popcorn kernels at the tips of the branches puffing open in the warmth of late spring. I'm anxious to start the herb garden—put in some basil plants, begin betting on pesto futures. But at this altitude the common wisdom is to wait until after Mother's Day when the chances of a late freeze are almost nil. Last year, my Italian and Thai basil thrived, both plants perfect green metaphors for their respective women. The Italian: voluptuous and rounded, sweetly pungent, carrying thick rosaries of white flowers. The Thai: slim tapering leaves, exotic anise fragrance and flavor, lotus-pink blossom spindles. It should have had waist-length ropes of black hair.

A woman passes,
soap scent fresh from the shower.
The breezes of May.

A tarantula was caught in the college library. If I had eight eyes, I could make short work of the stacks, maybe even get through the pile of books beside my bed that's been mulching there for years. It must be arachnid season. We saw a herd of tarantulas crossing a rural road like a flow of bristly black oil, then found one in our driveway when we got home— big enough that I expected to hear a sound like slow tires on gravel. They're relatively harmless—not that I want to wake up with one on my chest. I haven't seen tarantulas on our property before, though that doesn't mean they're not there. The animal tracks I find circumnavigating the house every morning remind me that the night still belongs to the critters. Such a false notion of ownership: the scat that peppers my land is as viable a deed as anything from the county recorder.

High desert darkness
devours all light but the moon's—
too big to swallow.

I teach my students that in a story *something* has to happen. It can't just be "and then, and then, and then." We all want continuity, defined arc, respite from the world's intrusions, assurance that things will work out just fine. That's what keeps religions in business. But would constant contentment be as boring to live as it is to read? Someone theorized that happiness can never be continuous (as it seems in some lives the opposite can); it only comes in spurts, like a brief bop riff before returning to the melody line. The secret, I think, is to recognize happiness while it's there. But does acknowledging happiness doom it, shrink it faster than a handful of ice cubes on a hard-on? I'd like to give it a try—uninterrupted happiness, not the ice.

Cat curled in the sun,
adrift upon pools of light;
pleasure where it's found.

Things can always get worse and generally will, which is the driving plot device in the darkest noirs. It seems this concept applies as well to scorpions. Once you find one, you know there are more. The first one we saw was trapped between the office windowpane and screen; it was very much alive, tail coiled and waving, until picked up with kitchen tongs then smashed with a hammer. That became the operative technique for dispatching the ones found in the laundry pile, the bedroom closet, and the garage . These were the little amber ones, which are more venomous than their larger relatives. Kind of like state legislators compared to U.S. Senators. The pest control guy told me to get a UV light. It seems scorpions are as fluorescent under black light as a Fillmore poster from my hippie days. But what if we flicked on the UV and they were...*everywhere?*

Political tips:
shake out your shoes each morning;
careful where you step.

PR reports that radioactive wild boars are running rampant in southern Germany. This is, in essence, Corman and Cronenberg territory. In actuality, it's Mad King Ludwig territory. But even a royal obsession with Wagner's operas ("the worst music ever invented," according to poet Philip Levine) can't set Geiger counters chattering. It takes a steady diet of Chernobyl (yes, still) fallout-infused truffles and mushrooms to do that.

Nuclear Valkyries
ride pigs instead of horses;
half-life leitmotif.

The glow-in-the-dark boars have been crashing buildings and homes, rapidly becoming more public danger than nuisance. Day or night, it doesn't matter; these beasts are their own headlights. Hunters can't shoot the boars fast enough, despite state bounties. And there just isn't that much demand for *wilde schwein* sausage, given dubious government tolerances for radiation-tainted meat. Humans can't eat their way out of this one.

Modest proposal:
Send radioactive food;
End third-world hunger.

We're not talking nasty Arizona javelinas here— European boars are hundreds of pounds of bristling pork on the hoof with attitude to spare and tusks that can gut a dog or tear open any human appendage within snorting distance. I hope the Black Forest hasn't been clear-cut; Bavarian locals are going to need some trees to climb.

Chain reaction greed;
we have laid waste wilderness—
toothpicks, boats, and doors.

Something moved in the brush while we were out for a walk, a lurking black and white. "Well," I whispered, "it's either a cat, a skunk, or a zebra and I think we can safely rule out one of those." We crept closer trying not to flush the creature or send it deeper under cover only to find our "animal" was a shredded piece of dirty plastic sheeting caught in the lower branches of a manzanita. So much for our sighting. Exactly when does imagination bow to reality? How many little cubes of sensory weight have to be piled on the scale? Where's the tipping point? My mother's Alzheimer's had a tipping point. I sometimes wonder if I ever got that dreaded diagnosis would I be able to sense the farthest, faintest calibration line of my self-awareness, the precise allowable angle of lean before the disease takes full control and my comprehension topples. This construct's so fragile, silk threads so fine; we only see half of what we see.

Web defined by dew;
design but no designer.
Spider's not at home.

The rock formations on our hike look similar to those distinctive jumbles that signify Joshua Tree in the California Mojave—pink granite masses that scrape the heels of your hands as you scramble to climb them for a better view. My wife and I talk about how we want to landscape the area in front of our house, how nice it would look to put a couple of big boulders beside our driveway surrounded by spiky native plants. We were shocked recently to find out how expensive rocks are to buy and place, and laugh again at the story of a local homeowner who spent thousands to put one giant specimen inside his patio walls. In this country, we pay for rocks; some people, that's all they've got.

Winds, wildfires, and floods;
I have no right to complain.
Trees down everywhere.

There's some confusion locally about Mingus Mountain. One source states it was named for two brothers, Joseph and Jacob Mingus, who owned a sawmill in the 1880s in northern Arizona's Black Hills, not far from Sedona. Another source disagrees, says it was named for William Mingus, an earlier prospector in the area. Personally, I think it should be renamed for Charles Mingus, the virtuoso jazz player. In fact, all number of American national landmarks should be named after jazz icons. How about Mt. Monk instead of Whitney? You don't get any higher than that in the contiguous United States. Why not Davis Delta for the Mississippi's fertile muted end? Coltrane Canyon would be a fitting tribute to two of America's wonders, both grand in their own ways. And shouldn't there be a Parker National Wildlife Refuge located along a major migratory flyway? Somewhere, too, there has to be Chet Baker Falls. But my choice is to rename Niagara, the big band of water features, for Ellington. One note, one vote—it's the American way.

Mountain summer jazz:
Woodpecker on percussion,
Cicada on bass.

Can't re-furl a leaf,
reverse the slide to autumn.
No hesitation.

Tony Bennett gives a radio interview promoting his new album, which features a duet with Amy Winehouse, dead at 27 soon after the session. It's early in the morning and I'm half-asleep listening with my eyes closed as a short sample of the cut is played. She sounds amazing, like Billie Holiday only more so. The interviewer comments that as Bennett is listening in the studio he's slowly shaking his head. I realize I'm doing the same in bed. "She had the gift," Bennett says. Yes, she did, I think. But she gave it back.

A lone swan floating,
there among brown pelicans.
Who really belongs?

The bees are not happy. I'm picking-back my basil plants that have gone to flower suddenly in this late heat. Basil honey...how would that taste? I have to wait until almost sunset after the agitated bees have gone back to the hive. Tomorrow morning when the bees return they'll buzz my plucked plants in confusion. I've taken away their livelihood, their means of production. No going back to school for re-training; this is what they do, have always done. I'm agribusiness and they're family farmers. They'll have to find another source of pollen. Say, that bush over there the hummingbirds love.

Bumblebees working,
bending red salvia stems.
Such weighty matters!

"I 've never gotten a tattoo," my sister says. She pulls up her sleeve and points to her wrist. "It reminds me too much of the Holocaust." I've toyed with the idea of tattoos but couldn't decide what symbol could define me for life. Too permanent on an impermanent body. Like everything else, tattoos and trends fade, though hate seems indelible. I read a newspaper piece about an incident in northern New Mexico: "Three Farmington men used a heated coat hanger to brand a swastika onto the arm of a mentally challenged Navajo man." In Sedona trading posts there are vintage Navajo rugs woven with swastikás— an ancient design hijacked forever by Hitler. A brand is another kind of tattoo that shows possession. Who's possessed in this case?

Twin bolts of lightning;
sudden summer storm enshrouds
Hokusai's Fuji.

orld peace. Or at least a glimpse of it from the hummingbird perspective. As monsoon season wanes, five hummingbirds sip at once: their wings remarkably stilled, busy little beaks and tongues. They fight dizzying, feather-jostling air wars for the right to a share from the feeder and now they're taking what's theirs. I hear billions are missing and unaccounted for in the Iraq war, Afghanistan, too; pallets of fresh currency handed out flagrantly, indiscriminately, to dark operatives, shady government connections, newly-minted contractors, and the vile former vice president's octopus-armed cronies— carpetbaggers reincarnated from our own civil war, still grabbing.

New democracies:
graft flies black helicopters,
American made.

Sewage runs in the streets of once-viable Iraqi towns; electricity is still an iffy commodity even after all these dollars and years. Premature babies placed in threesomes in duct tape-patched incubators while parents forage black markets to fetch drugs for doctors who have none. No one's been prosecuted: those who were in power, who fabricated the war, don't apologize. It's all water under the al-Sarrafiyah Bridge, they say. Let's look to the future, they say, which for them include Georgetown townhouses, estates in Virginia or Connecticut or Maryland.

The river of lies;
pockets filled with Tigris silt
leak a trail back home.

There's water on the moon. The shores of all those poetically-named *maria* someday could be beachfront property, Cancun-style resorts wedged among the craters. Moon rocks from years ago are the evidence; tests we didn't have in the Apollo era now show aqueous chemical traces, and reports of ice dust backwash at lunar landing sites have been confirmed. In some boardroom plans probably are being made for plunder when our terrestrial resources are squandered and we're running dry. The moon is full tonight, harvest orange rising with Jupiter star-like at its side. All that green cheese to eat and now we know there's something to wash it down.

The October moon—
Jupiter has sixty-three,
yet we're rich with one.

*C*lothes shopping with my wife, I lose interest, say I'm going over to the men's department to look around. So much skull merchandise. As if Death needs a logo. As if Death needs to advertise. Death: the designer—jewelry, T-shirts, belt buckles, even shoes. Thank goodness there's no signature fragrance. Does wearing grinning skulls show you're not afraid, that you're too cool to care, that you laugh into its hollow sockets? Does it mean you support its team? Death and his agents seem busier than ever. My daughter, Jade, sobs on the phone that suddenly people around her are seriously ill. I think of those close to me, failing, dying, wish I could offer more comfort. She's just now learning the bittersweet toast: "To absent friends…"

Farmer's Market sign:
"Hurry! The season's last crop."
This fleeting summer…

The blue Toyota sports a bumper sticker: "US Navy Seals 1, Osama bin Laden 0." While I understand the patriotic swagger of the statement, I question its accuracy. At the very least I have to insist upon an asterisk next to it, as for a qualified baseball record. Yes, it's true that the Seals did conduct a daring raid on a compound inside Pakistan and took out America's number-one enemy, plus a wife or two and a few armed bit players. But is Osama's score really zero? After that asterisk a footnote has to read: Nearly 3,000 dead in the World Trade Center and Pentagon attacks and crash of Flight 93; untold soldiers and civilians dead and still dying plus collateral maiming of families; the ongoing erosion of U.S. rights and privacies in the name of "national security"; billions and billions spent on mendacious presidential vendettas dressed in the uniforms of foreign wars while America sputters and bickers over lack of funds and cutbacks; and, at the very least, the end of air travel being fun. Those are massive consequences directly linked to a guy with a doughnut after his name on the scoreboard. And about that "burial at sea"...

Wilted red flowers.
No, balloons snagged in hedges.
Whose party's over?

Cactus wrens nesting,
saguaro symbiosis.
No mortgage needed.

U rban sprawl has become suburban sprawl has become rural sprawl. Even the land bridges between outlying malls are disappearing. People think *we* live in the sticks 12 miles outside town, but we have paved roads and sewers, neighbors close enough that we can see them on their patios, smell their grilling. Granted, it's not like the new complexes, houses built to the limits of lots, where you can reach out one kitchen window and into another. Then there are the zombie subdivisions south of Phoenix where construction just stopped mid-hammer blow: stalled shopping centers with store signs in place, parking space lines painted. And across the street, the raw plywood and joists of unfinished McMansions, xeriscape abandoned, pools unfilled. Homeowners and speculators there got so far underwater they just put on fins and snorkels, swam away across the bank-owned desert.

ometimes trying to raise the living is harder than trying to raise the dead. You'd think with email/voicemail/cellphones/iPads/Skype, even retro landlines, I could reach someone to talk to. But no. Not at the moment. Nobody's around. And speaking of raising the dead, I read that in Los Angeles waste management workers have to go through more than 3,000 tons of recycling a month looking for crime victims and, especially, the homeless, who expire in rubbish bins while seeking food and shelter. When it comes to our bodies, recycling is mandatory.

Those empty houses,
snail shell and rattlesnake skin:
strategic defaults.

My daughter's bio appears on her new employer's web site. She's in the big river now— impossible deadlines, oblivious managers, demanding clients, sniping co-workers. Oh yeah, it's all there skulking low behind her cubicle's coarse fabric walls as she wolfs down lunch at her desk. She complains about having no time for herself anymore, that all she does is go home and crash, brain dead TV and bed. Then back to work again. I feel her pain. But when I remind her I did 25 years, my words turn brittle in my mouth as if someone left shards of shell in the egg salad. I once overheard a friend say to his young daughter, "Work is no fun. That's why they pay you to do it." It bears repeating. But I don't.

Four seasons of work,
two weeks vacation a year.
Boss crow stealing eggs.

The dot.com advertises that it can protect you from "viruses, hackers, spam, and cyberthreats"—the four riders of the new Apocalypse. What is it about the number four? There are four seasons and four movements in Beethoven's Fifth, four quarters in a football game and what used to be a dollar. Native Americans have four sacred directions and Passover has the Four Questions. But the Chinese think the number four unlucky because its written character is the same as for death, even though Internet crime and crashes didn't exist at the time their language evolved. The Japanese are also wary; *Ikebana* arrangements are based on threes. The Great Pyramid at Giza has four sides, too, sloping in and up, pointing to the eye that hovers above it on our money. You know, the all-seeing eye that never blinks, like the security cameras that are everywhere.

No privacy, just
going about your business.
Skunk waddles across.

You have two choices
in political parties:
toilet or sewer.

The "Arab Spring" has come and gone. Tunisia, Egypt, Libya—one oppressor after another deposed, one country after another "liberated" into democracy. We'll see how that works out. Back in the late 1960s we protested the Vietnam war and got beaten, tear gassed, and arrested. At Kent State protesters got shot, like in Syria, Bahrain, and Iran. I remember at the time overhearing one Ohio State professor say to another, "I hope they kill a few more." In Oakland, the cops waded in with clubs, rubber bullets, and "non-lethal projectiles" against an Occupy crowd in a park massing against financial inequality, government inaction, and corporate immunity. The demonstrators also wanted to save the jobs of public employees, such as police; the irony was lost on the officers. We should be grateful tanks weren't used as in Tiananmen Square, Prague, and in spring, 1932, Washington DC, when the veterans Bonus Army occupied parks in the other Depression demanding what was promised them.

Occupy this math:
Ninety-nine percent of nothing
still equals nothing.

I f you're poor: it's your fault. If you worry that you're one illness away from bankruptcy: too bad. If you lost your job: take a number. If you *have* a job but lie awake nights waiting for the centipede shoes to drop: not our problem. If you're unemployed and can't find work because there's bias against those who've been let go: buckle down. If your benefits have run out and your premiums were raised: hey, it's just business. If you're over 50, lotsa luck; it's not that bad living with your kids. Your call is important to us so please listen carefully as options have changed: Push 1 for English, 2 for indifference, 3 for desperation.

If you are hungry,
work harder at weaving a
better web, spider.

If you are homeless,
you should have constructed a
better nest, sparrow.

Venice Beach. The September sun comes down like a steel grate. Walking back on Speedway, one lane, one way, I'm passed in quick succession by a Maserati, a Lexus, and a BMW 7. The shiny black cars are partying tonight. At home I flip through my wife's magazines—*Elle, In Style, Vogue:* page after page of half-dressed twenty-something starlets, models with filly legs, kohl eyes, and scowls. I'm invisible to them. I play the dad in the series. I play the dad in real life. I should be thankful for what I have. I wish I couldn't remember what I'll never have again.

Her peach freckled skin;
searching for constellations,
connecting the dots.

There were two dogs and a stag with antlers and early snow clouds on the horizon. Something large was dead on the shoulder of the road. As I drew near I saw it was a bear lying on its back, paws in the air. The bear had beige fur frosted with white and I remember wondering how it had died. The dogs ran up to investigate the bear, with Tania trailing behind, weaving among the swath of trees that lined the empty highway. The stag stood beside me and I stroked its neck. I knew it was there to protect me. Then the bear shuddered, rolled onto its belly, blinking and slowly shaking its head. It had only been sleeping and now Tania and the dogs were too close. The bear rose to its full height and spread its forelimbs, the claws at the ends of its paws as long as terminal feathers on redtail wings. Silhouetted against the gray sky it was huge. I yelled to Tania, *Get back!* But she couldn't hear me or see the bear through the branches, didn't seem to fear any harm.

Stars still out at five,
darkness long this time of year;
asleep or awake.

AFTERWORD

I first encountered the *haibun* form in Gary Snyder's 2004 poetry collection, *Danger on Peaks*. I read and re-read Snyder's *haibun* and initially dismissed them as flat—certainly not what I had come to expect from such a remarkable poet of nature and spirit. Yet, the more I thought about Snyder's *haibun*, the more intrigued I became. And then I encountered another *haibun* poem in Robert Hass's Pulitzer Prize- and National Book Award-winning collection, *Time and Materials*. I realized that maybe the *haibun* form deserved more serious consideration if two of my poetry heroes were writing them. I think that poets and students of writing often can learn more from what they don't like than from what they do. So I began to investigate what, exactly, it was about *haibun* that at first confounded and later attracted me, and to try to understand the subtle craft inherent in how and why they work.

The roots of the *haibun* form were cultivated by Matsuo Bashō (1644-1694), as was so much of the Japanese poetry that followed him. Most Westerners know Bashō as a master—perhaps *the* master—of the haiku form. His haiku about the sound of a frog jumping into a pond may be the most famous, or at least the most repeated, haiku of all time. Bashō primarily worked in haiku and in linked *renga* verse, but also wrote in the more prose-like and allusive *haibun* style. Inquiry into the *haibun* form inevitably leads to Bashō's late masterpiece, *Narrow Road to the Interior*. From title to text this little gem of a book is a marvel of metaphor masquerading as a travel journal with entries written in *haibun*. On the surface the book chronicles a journey Bashō began in the spring/summer of 1689 with his friend Sora. Disguised as Zen monks for protection from bandits, they penetrated into the northern interior of Japan. But as becomes clear, the physical countryside was not the only "interior" being explored; Bashō also was venturing into his own interior landscape.

For me, writing *haibun* was just a matter of making myself sit down and give it a go, to springboard from the style and tone of Bashō and try to imitate the form as best I could. I felt like an art student in a museum with a drawing pad copying the Old Masters. As with most poetry forms, *haibun* are more difficult to write than they seem, especially achieving the detached, yet introspective, sensibility of Bashō's work. The most difficult part for me was overcoming the impulse to poetry and poetic language. But after awhile I found myself responding creatively to everything in *haibun/* haiku form. By the time I finished this manuscript, I was beginning to worry whether I'd ever be able to write lyric free verse again.

As stated in the "Introduction" to this collection, my *haibun* are approximations—more specifically, appropriations—of the form. My haiku also are not traditionally exact and probably never could be. Even Snyder does not consider his haiku to be true haiku. In a brief verbal exchange I had with him about the *haibun* form, he kept correcting my use of the term haiku in reference to his work. What he writes to accompany the *haibun* prose blocks, he insisted, are "short poems." So, in deference to Snyder's definition, what I have in *52 Views* are poems written in the manner of *haibun*. But isn't that how every art evolves—an artist or writer standing on the shoulders of all those who have gone before, pushing the boundaries of established forms and adding something of their own.

Most of these *haibun* were written while I was living in the high desert mountains of Prescott, Arizona, dealing with four distinct seasons (including cold, snowy winters) after 30-plus years of pretty much daily perfect weather in coastal Los Angeles.

Given the seasonal references of classic haiku, it was the ideal setting. The events that jump-started these *haibun* were bookended between the winters of 2010 and 2011, making it a journal of sorts (in keeping with Bashō's journaling), with later *haibun* added as inspiration and events prompted. They're presented in the order they were written, although occasionally a little poetic license was invoked for the sake of pacing.

However, upon further review (as they used to say in my NFL days), the provenance of this collection probably dates to March, 2008, when my wife, Tania, and I went to visit my daughter, Jade, a Japanese language major doing her junior year abroad in Kyoto. Like Bashō, we traveled north, cleverly disguised as *gaijin* tourists, lucky to have the advantage of Jade's fluency. As a special treat, Jade had booked two nights for us at a *ryokan* beside Lake Kawaguchi in the shadow of Mt. Fuji. I expected a traditional rural Japanese inn, all dark wood, sliding doors, and meditative inner gardens. But the cab from the train station delivered us to an upscale modern hotel. Yes, there were futons laid out for us at night that were discretely rolled and put away while we were at breakfast. But our *ryokan* also featured a roof spa and heated infinity pool facing the mountain. It was so overcast when we arrived I despaired I'd never see Fuji except for what was visible beneath the clouds draped low from across its shoulders. Then the kimono fell open, so to speak. The weather turned clear and glorious, and there was Mt. Fuji in all its symmetrical snowcapped magnificence, perfectly reflected and reversed in the suddenly still water of the lake. I had an odd sensation that I had seen that scene before, not exactly "woo-woo" past-life déjà-vu, but maybe in one of the dozens of samurai movies I've watched. It wasn't until weeks after I got home that I discovered why the scene was familiar. Leafing through one of my most prized art books, Hokusai's *The Thirty-six Views of Mt. Fuji*, I came across the very lake-side vision of the "upside down Fuji" I'd seen—or at least Hokusai's interpretation of it done as a woodblock print more than 180 years earlier.

So the title of this poetry collection is a direct reference to that series of *ukiyo-e* prints created by Katsushika Hokusai (1760-1849)—a visual travelogue that orbits around Japan's highest mountain. Hokusai's iconic "wave" print (officially titled "Great Wave Off the Coast of Kanagawa") is from this Mt. Fuji series, and is to *ukiyo-e* specifically, and Japanese art in general, what Bashō's little frog poem is to haiku. Also like Bashō, Hokusai was an innovator in his art, taking *ukiyo-e* images beyond the more usual portraits of courtesans and Kabuki actors into depictions of landscape with perspective, a surprisingly novel *ukiyo-e* concept at the time. I've always loved Japanese *ukiyo-e* woodblock prints as much for the poetry in the translation of the term *ukiyo-e*—"Pictures of the Floating World"—as for their actual images. In the case of Hokusai's Lake Kawaguchi *ukiyo-e*, it's not the world that's floating but the mountain.

The prints in Hokusai's *Thirty-six Views* series were primarily published and sold between 1826 and 1833. (In an interesting timeline crossover, John James Audubon was selling the hand-colored engravings from his *Birds of America* series by subscription at about the same time.) When Hokusai reached the final thirty-sixth print in his series, demand for the work was still high. So Hokusai and his publisher did what any enterprising artist and businessman would do—they ignored the series title and continued producing views of Fuji. But then the younger Utagawa Hiroshige entered the art market around 1832 with his *Fifty-three Stages of the Tokaido*, a series of *ukiyo-e* depicting scenic stops along the road from Edo (Tokyo) to then-Imperial capital Kyoto (sort of Tokugawa Japan's version of U.S. Route 66), and his work may have become the "next big thing" for print collectors of the period. Hokusai's sales dropped, and he stopped adding to the *36 Views* series after producing 46 prints in all.

My original intention was to write 36 *haibun* and collect them in a chapbook entitled *36 Views*. But when I hit 36 *haibun* more kept coming and, further imitating Hokusai, I continued. Hence, the 52 *haibun* in this book, and *52 Views*. As all poets know, you don't question when you're given a poem; you just say "Thank you."

Which brings me to the Philosopher's Walk mentioned in the "Introduction." On my last day with Jade in Kyoto we visited that popular path that links the Nanzen-ji and Ginkaku-ji temples and where Kyoto University philosophy professor Nishida Kitaro (1870-1945) is said to have taken daily walks "lost in thought." Jade and I strolled the path along the small canal together in intermittent rain, surrounded by women in kimonos and a multi-colored profusion of umbrellas mimicking the fresh blossoms on seemingly every bush and tree. It was such a transcendent experience we walked the path's length back and forth three times. In my (un-numbered) view, it was one of the best days of my life ●

Jim Natal
Marina del Rey, California
November, 2012

NOTES

Epigraph
The haiku that opens *52 Views* accompanies a *haibun* in Bashō's *Narrow Road to the Interior*, translated by Sam Hamill.

Preparing for winter
The poem mentioned in the *haibun* is "A Guest Doesn't Come" by Chinese Tang Dynasty poet Po Chu-i (772-846):

Candleflame red and wine clear, I settle in and just wait.
At dawn's first light, I'm wandering in and out the gate,

stars thin and moon drifting low. No guest. Night's now
sunrise lost in willow mist, a magpie taking flight, gone.

(translated by David Hinton in *The Selected Poems of Po Chu-i*)

I had to bring in the potted cacti is for N.D.

My wife and I down with infection
Buddha's first noble truth: Life is suffering.

Winter storm warnings
The last line quotes a wonderfully mysterious and evocative haiku by Yosa Buson (1716-1783):

Tethered horse;
snow
in both stirrups.

(translated by Robert Hass in *The Essential Haiku*)

An NFL head coach
The mangled sayings are quotes from Joe Kuharich, who coached the Philadelphia Eagles from 1964-1968.

The haiku quotes a line from Witter Bynner's 1944 translation of Lao Tzu's *The Way of Life*, section 12: "The race, the hunt, can drive men mad..."

Something moved in the brush and **If you're poor**
The short poems following these *haibun* are nods to two of my
favorite haiku, both featuring spiders. The first is by Bashō and
the second is by Kobayashi Issa (1763-1827), a later haiku
master nearly (in my opinion) Bashō's equal:

With what voice,
and what song would you sing, spider,
in this autumn breeze?

(translated by R.H. Blyth in his four-volume set Haiku)

Don't worry, spiders,
I keep house
casually.

(translated by Robert Hass in *The Essential Haiku*)

There's some confusion locally is for Gerald McDermott

There's water on the moon
Lunar *maria* are dark plains on the moon formed by ancient
volcanic eruptions. Early astronomers thought them to be seas,
hence the name *mare/maria*, Latin for "sea(s)."

The short poem following this *haibun* is an homage to a haiku
by Oshima Ryota (1718-1787):

Tonight's moon!
Unthinkable
that there is only one!

(translated by R.H. Blyth in his four-volume set Haiku)

Afterword
In 1834, Hokusai, at the age of 74 and still competitive as
an artist, began publishing a brand new series of prints, *One
Hundred Views of Mount Fuji*, more than double the number he
created for *Thirty-Six Views*. In the preface to this late series,
Hokusai (as translated by Charles S. Terry) wrote: "After I was
about half a hundred, I often published pictures, but until I was
seventy, none of them was really worth anything."

The books referenced in the "Afterword" are:

—*Narrow Road to the Interior*, Matsuo Bashō, translated by Sam Hamill, Shambhala Publications, Inc, Boston, MA, 1991.

—My book of Hokusai's *The Thirty-Six Views of Mt. Fuji*, is one volume of a two-book boxed set, *Two Great Masters of Ukiyo-e*, published by East-West Center Press in 1965 that also includes Hiroshige's *The Fifty-three Stages of the Tokaido*. It features introductory text by the late Ichitaro Kondo, with an English adaptation by Charles S. Terry.

TEBOT BACH
A 501 (c) (3) Literary Arts Education Non Profit

THE TEBOT BACH MISSION: advancing literacy, strengthening community, and transforming life experiences with the power of poetry through readings, workshops, and publications.

THE TEBOT BACH PROGRAMS

1. A poetry reading and writing workshop series for venues such as homeless shelters, battered women's shelters, nursing homes, senior citizen daycare centers, Veterans organizations, hospitals, AIDS hospices, correctional facilities which serve under-represented populations. Participating poets include: John Balaban, Brendan Constantine, Megan Doherty, Richard Jones, Dorianne Laux, M.L. Leibler, Laurence Lieberman, Carol Moldaw, Patricia Smith, Arthur Sze, Carine Topal, Cecilia Woloch.

2. A poetry reading and writing workshop series for the community Southern California at large, and for schools K-University. The workshops feature local, national, and international teaching poets; David St. John, Charles Webb, Wanda Coleman, Amy Gerstler, Patricia Smith, Holly Prado, Dorothy Lux, Rebecca Seiferle, Suzanne Lummis, Michael Datcher, B.H. Fairchild, Cecilia Woloch, Chris Abani, Laurel Ann Bogen, Sam Hamill, David Lehman, Christopher Buckley, Mark Doty.

3. A publishing component to give local, national, and international poets a venue for publishing and distribution.

Tebot Bach
Box 7887
Huntington Beach, CA 92615-7887
714-968-0905
www.tebotbach.org

This book is set in 12 point Bembo.

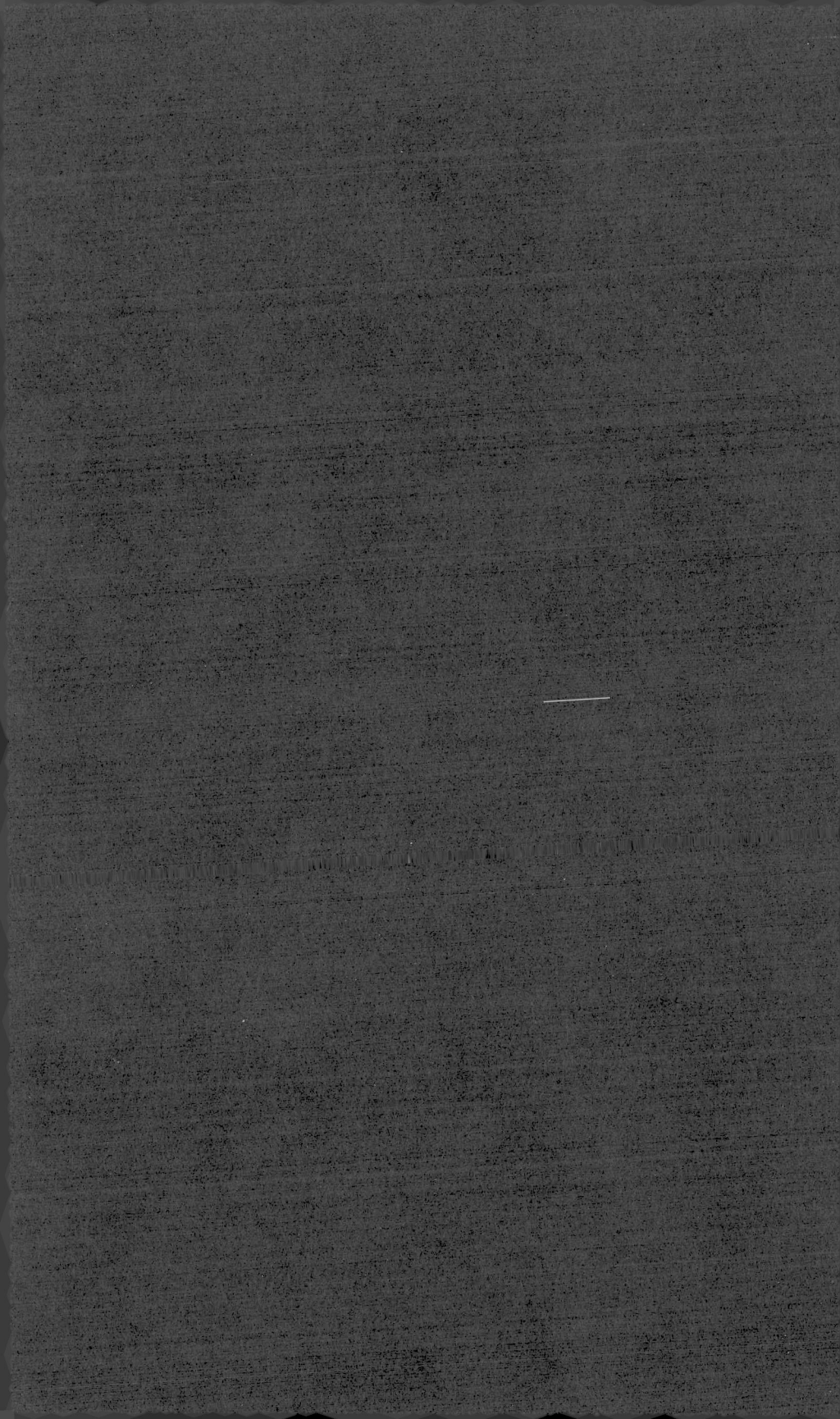